Poet Tree
Root, Branch & Sap

PHILLIP A. ROSS

Marietta, Ohio

Copyright ©2013 Phillip A. Ross
All rights reserved.

ISBN: 978-0-9839046-5-6
Edition: 2020.09.13

Published by

Pilgrim Platform
149 E. Spring St.,
Marietta, Ohio, 45750
www.pilgrim-platform.org

Printed in the United States of America

Cover photos of Phillip A. Ross: left: high school (1965) and right: seminary (1980

*For Too Many Friends
Along the Journey
Too Long Forgotten*

Books by Phillip A. Ross

The Work At Zion—A Reckoning, Two-volume set, 772 pages, 1996.
Practically Christian—Applying James Today, 135 pages, 2006.
The Wisdom of Jesus Christ in the Book of Proverbs, 414 pages, 2006.
Marking God's Word—Understanding Jesus, 324 pages, 2006.
Acts of Faith—Kingdom Advancement, 326 pages, 2007.
Informal Christianity—Refining Christ's Church, 136 pages, 2007.
Engagement—Establishing Relationship in Christ, 104 pages, 1996, 2008.
It's About Time! — The Time Is Now, 40 pages. 2008.
The Big Ten—A Study of the Ten Commandments, 105 pages, 2001, 2008.
Arsy Varsy—Reclaiming The Gospel in First Corinthians, 406 pages, 2008.
Varsy Arsy—Proclaiming The Gospel in Second Corinthians, 356 pages, 2009.
Colossians—Christos Singularis, 278 pages, 2010.
Rock Mountain Creed—The Sermon on the Mount, 310 pages, 2011.
The True Mystery of the Mystical Presence, 355 pages, 2011.
Peter's Vision of Christ's Purpose in First Peter, 340 pages, 2011.
Peter's Vision of The End in Second Peter, 184 pages, 2012.
The Religious History of Nineteenth Century Marietta, Thomas Jefferson Summers, 124 pages, 1903, 2012 (editor).
Conflict of Ages—The Great Debate of the Moral Relations of God and Man, Edward Beecher, 489 pages, 1853, 2012 (editor).
Concord Of Ages—The Individual And Organic Harmony Of God And Man, Edward Beecher, D. D., 524 pages, 1860, 2013 (editor).
Ephesians—Recovering the Vision of a Sustainable Church in Christ, 417 pages, 2013.
Galatians: Backstory/Christory, 315 pages, 2015.
Poet Tree—Root, Branch & Sap, 72 pages, 2013.
Inside Out Woman—Collected Poetry, Doris M. Ross, 195 pages, 2014 (editor).
God's Great Plan for the World—The Biblical Story of Creation and Redemption, 305 pages, 2019.
John's Miracles—Seeing Beyond Our Expectations, 210 pages, 2019.
Essays on Church—Ordinary Christianity for the World, 385 pages, 2020.

Table of Contents

Introduction..1
Show Me...5
Rain..7
Distance..8
Mortal..9
Land Mine...10
A Bus Ride..12
Morning / Mourning......................................13
Home...15
For Ears That See..16
To Love..17
Bidin' Time...21
O death..23
A Christmas Story..24
Finding is Lost..26
Devotion..28
Come With Me...29
Can It Be Me?...30
Friday Night...31
Mr. Straight...32
Everybody...33
Children!...34
Comin' Home...35
Huh?..37
On Magic..40
Rock On..41
The Law of Universal War............................42
64,000..43
To Whom I May Concern.............................44

Prolepses..46
Lost Again..47
Kidd Tit...48
Tune Up..51
Some Koan..53
One X One / One = One................................54
Hoo?...56
A sketchy Portrait...57
The Obvious...62
An Experience of Grace..................................63
The Confessional..66
Alphalogos..67
Cherries..68
Christ Across!...69
Jesus' Prayer..70
The Lord Also Snows.....................................71
Trinitarianism...73
Unitarianism...74

Introduction

My mother was an avid reader. I have fond memories of her cooking—stirring with one hand and a book in the other. She really wasn't a very good cook, but she was a very good reader. She read her weight in books every year. For my sixteenth birthday she bought me *The Encyclopedia of Ancient and Forbidden Knowledge*, a very fat, juicy book with a forbidding cover. She made me the reader that I am, and gave me a thirst for knowledge.

Dad was a debater. He loved to argue. And he was a raving extrovert, friendly enough to argue with strangers. He'd argue B to your A, or D to your C—it didn't seem to matter what the argument was about. It was the engagement that fired his passion. He was a true seeker of truth. However, he sought it in all the wrong places, but that's another story.

There were five kids in my family. I am the oldest son. We lived in a three bedroom house with one bathroom. We always thought we were normal, middle-class people, and we were. Both of my parents had been divorced before they married, and divorced again after twenty-seven years. Both brought children into the marriage. Dad brought Jackie, my older sister, and mom brought me. Scott and Sara are twins, and David is the youngest.

My childhood was dominated by mediocrity. I was an average kid in an average house with an average family in an average school with average friends. I graduated right in the middle of my thousand member senior high school class. I didn't play sports, or an instrument in the band. Never ran for office or did to any extracurricular activities. And never took any formal lessons.

Nonetheless, the Lord spoke to me one day. It was a Sunday. We lived kitty-corner from the church. I was twelve, and the Sunday School lesson had been on God's forgiveness. Apparently, God forgave everyone of everything, at least that's pretty much what I heard from our elderly and very kind Sunday School teacher. She'd taken a shine to me for some unknown reason.

Bobby Walker was my nemesis. He was a greaser, I was a nerd. He was a year ahead of me in school, but we were in the same Sunday School class. He was a head taller than me. After class that Sunday he put me in a headlock in the hall and gave me a knuckle rub.

"Yea, Ross! You gotta forgive me!" Peals of laughter barked out of the mouths of his friends.

My head was throbbing as I walked home, across the street. It was a beautiful Spring day, the sun was shining and the air was crisp.

"How in the world can I forgive a guy like Bobby Walker?" I thought. "God must be something to be able to forgive everyone." Before the thought was finished the answer slapped me across the brain.

"God has infinite forgiveness. So, when people run out, they can just ask and He'll give 'em more." I don't remember the actual words, but they don't really matter. The idea rang clear and true, and I knew it was the real answer.

I remember thinking, "Wow!" I had no other response. The rest of the day played out as usual, and I told no one of my conversation with God. But I have never forgotten it because I also learned that day that I could talk to God anytime. He and I were on speaking terms. He told me true stuff. But that idea was so weird that I could share it with no one. So I didn't.

I began a conversation with God that day that has not stopped. Much later I learned to call it *prayer*. But I never really liked what I learned about prayer. It seemed so artificial, stiff, and formal—awkward really. It was a lot easier to dispense with the formalities and just talk to God in the privacy of my own head.

So, my poetry—which was written pretty early in my life, though I also wrote as an adult—is mostly brief snippets of our talks. It's not all that profound, though it likes to pretend differently. And you need to know in advance that I have a wry sense of humor. So does God, and maybe that's why we get along. If humor is funny because it contrasts odd things in unexpected ways, then the best humor isn't all that funny. It's weird! The best humor is ridiculously weird. I often say that I'm *half joking*. My wife calls it *joking on the square*.

Mostly, my poetry is just raw emotion looking for a connection, an idea looking for a place to be. Like most poetry it sings lonely songs decorated with hopeful expectations. Too much of it is existential angst tinged with silliness. Honestly, it's an embarrassment to me now, but it's also real. There were too many years of self-reflection before I stopped wallowing in it.

Like too many poets, I found that life can be painful. And I mistook much of the pain for meaning. It was only much later as I came to Christ, or came to grips with life—they are the same things, functionally—that I quit writing poetry. Then again, maybe I didn't quit, but just switched to prose. But poetry broke out now and then anyway. It has a voice of its own.

It is what it is, part of my life. So here is some of it.

Phillip A. Ross
Marietta, Ohio
March 2013

Show Me

Morning has come and hung the sun.
  My dreams begin to blur, thoughts stir.

If I could be anything
If I could do anything
There is to do—
I'd do you.

I think I'll play in the park today
  Will you be there?
  How long must we play hide and seek
Before you let me see your secret smile?
  How long must my face be drawn
Before the dawn?

How long?
I can shine.
Be mine.

I saw it in your face
  Again tonight.
I saw it in your eyes
  As they sparkled and spied
  And tried to hide
  Again tonight.

It was in your walk
  The way you sway
The way you say hello
  Was there again.

I've seen it before
  It was there before you
And it was there before her
  And before that
  And after her
  And after you.

But I saw it
  In your face
  Tonight.

Rain

I

A dash through the rain
  Up the stair to the door,
I cut through the blackened room
  To the silent sound of soft breathing.

II

The rain rolls out a quiet roar
  Deep into the starless night,
My love lies naked along my side
  In silent sleep.
My lips touch her warm cheek,
  And I am again absorbed
Into the dark, quiet roar
  Of the starless night.

III

Walking through the rain
  Sharing a small umbrella,
Hand in hand
  Splashing through muddy puddles
Soaking wet
  Sharing, laughing, loving.

Distance

Separated by a reality
That knows no love
Out of hands.

I lie alone
Wakesleeping thoughts of
My memories of you.

    Love is
A rainbow so magnificent
  God looks up.

Our nakednesses touch
  Freefall
  In a
  Satin
  Lined
  Steaming
  Pass.i.o.n.

    I love your naked body
    With my naked body
      Our Flesh.

A word
Whispered
A thought

    Love.

1969

Mortal

A man died today
A man, whom everybody knew
  and everybody loved.
A man, who was lonely
A man, who was only
A boy
  at heart
A boy, who laughed and played and
  prayed and laid
A boy, who cried
  died
A man today.

1969

Land Mine

A wife, a lover, a woman
 bawls, physically
wretches for breath as if
 the very life were
being sucked out of her.

Clutching, quivering, spasmodically
 she rasps for air
and cries out like a wounded
 animal—even the dead
perk their ears.

You listen, I listen
 no comfort to give
kind words only irritate
 the wound.
O God! She convulses still.

His mother stares with
 hollow eyes.
Love, hatred, pity burning
 in her chest
silently screaming. No ... no!

A man who loved, who hated
 a man snuffed out.
God! A life, an entity
 blown to hell!
God? Merciful pitiful world!

A friend, a neighbor, his brother
 silently, lovingly

> take them, hold them, lead them
>   down the road—
> empty, staggering, sobbing.

1969

A Bus Ride

Dusk in the city.
I always ride home
   alone.
My nose in a book.

One eye reading
One eye watching
   the world.
A dream in my head.

A bent old man
   with a stick
Slowly climbs aboard.
He smiles at his audience,
And exhausted, plops
   into a seat.

Buses are for the old
   and the young,
   and the lonely.
It's a crowded, jostling
   lonely ride.

Smile mirrors smile.
I always ride home
   alone.

1969

MORNING / MOURNING

I don't want to
Have to leave you
'Cause I love you
And I love you
So I'll leave you
'Cause you want me to.

It hurts me so
Like I never
Hurt before
An' my heart is
Open, always bleedin'
So it's always hurtin'
And yet I want to go.

If I ever
Took your freedom an'
Didn't let you do
What you want to do
An' you wanted to
Then that's not love.

Yes, love is
Lovin' sure an'
It's givin' all you
Got and more
'Till your heart is sore
But that sure as hell ain't all.

I'd never clip your
Wings like
The men do

In the zoo
So the birds don't fly
With the settin' sun
But it hurts me so.

When we part our ways
In the chill of the morn
In the foggy haze
Remember that I care
An' always will.

Sure I'll be blue
But don't think I'm through
With life and livin'
There's a lot of givin'
I've got to do.

We had the all of love
An' did the things an'
Had the thrills an' quivered in
The warm heart an'
Throbbing thighs of love.

All that's left for
Me to do is fall upon
My knees an' pray an'
Plead that love give
You a loving life forevermore.

June 1969

Home

My kittens to love
   and hug
to feed—they purr
   and softly rub my
tired ankles with their backs.

I sleep alone
   and cold.
They do love me
   and sprawl all over
the crisp bed,
but I'm lonely.

1969

For Ears That See

The only way to successfully
control the machine is by
non-participation in it.
Live your own life, your own
way. The power is money.
Each of us as individuals
can limit that power by
participating in poverty.
Death is their end and tax
is their means. Boycott money.

1970

To Love

You were there
and I let you go
what did I know
your love was so near
I was almost here
oh, what did I know.

The story is old
and I was young
had the truth been told
no song to be sung
we had us, yes
we laughed and
we played, together
we stayed for a time
we were made one together
by that one that
is the one of all.

And then one day
you went away
my head, my love tumbled
spinning and turning.
I thought that I knew
but I was just learning.
Now my heart
has been glowing
for the knowing that
soon now you
will be returning.

And when my
silly head swells
with yearning and
my guts are turning
I can smile
knowing the seeds
that I'm sowing
belong to love
and because my love
is love my heart
will go on beating
in time.

1971

What could I do to let you see me?
What could I say to let you know?
The solitude of self is crying out
for company. The ocean of consciousness
is presently too vast—"faith!"
"Faith" is cried to me. "What is it
that you have no faith. If you have
faith the solitude will disappear—
fear not." I know now that love is
an illusion, ultimately. I desire
love, but I am love. There is no
need to desire what I am. The words
run together, no meaning. There is
a feeling that desires to feel.
Patience is needed. All of my words
run together into Om.

1971

During the time
Of my greatest need
I need so much
That I can't put it
Together to find
What I need most
Is help looking.

Bidin' Time

Lord knows I need you Jesus when
  I'm blue.
I need somewhere to turn, yes she said
  that we were thru.
Come on and fill my heart with the love
  that's always new.
Lord knows I need you Jesus, yes I do.

When you fill my heart, Lord, I know
  that it is right,
And all the eyes that mine do meet
  do shine with your delight.
Yes, I can fill them with your love
  warm them with your heat.

Every love of mind can shine
  like a fire in the night.
And when she goes away, Lord,
Yes, when she leaves me dry
I know your love still lights
  the northern sky.
Lord knows I need you Jesus,
  yes I do.

1970

All of life is a fervent embrace,
change and relationship
defined as love
is so difficult to realize.
Everything is relationship
and the control of it is
not ours alone.

1971

O death,

For so long now we have pushed you
aside. We have neglected and
ignored you. Soon you will ride
into our lives on your silver
chariot and reclaim your rightful
place among us. Yet we shall not
fear, for you are our salvation.

1971

A Christmas Story

Back in august of, oh, about 31 A.D. or so Jesus of Nazareth thought that there should be at least one special day during the week once a year. It could be a day, Jez' though, of rest and of relaxation. A day that nobody would have to work. Even mothers could slack off a little, if, say, they prepared the entire day's meals the night before and left the prepared meals in the oven at a low temperature to keep them warm; and, of course, if there were enough dishes in the house to last the day.

Now Jez' knew enough about institutions, organizations, and governments to know that they would not accept a special day holiday for no reason. The special day holiday needed a history, and Jesus knew it. He thought and thought.

"Christ!" Jesus thought, "if I write a Special Day Holiday history in script it would be indisputable." Up until this time nothing had been written, so who was to know what was what.

Jesus had no formal schooling to speak of. He had dropped out of the Temple when he was twelve. But he was very resourceful. He was also familiar with the long-standing custom of exchanging gifts at Birthmas. Jesus figured that on the Special Day Holiday everyone could give gifts to his very fat, jolly friend in red, Nick. Nick lived in the slums on E. 6th St. and could use a lot of gifts to boost his socioeconomic status, of which Nick was low.

Well, Jez' wrote down the Special Day Holiday history in script and he submitted it to all of the institutions, organizations and governments on the south side. His proposal was unanimously defeated and Jesus was sent to the North Pole in a sled as punishment for the pinko, leftist and undoubtedly communist-inspired proposal.

Three of the neighborhood smartalecs caught wind of this event and, as a public demonstration in the theater of the absurd, send Nick some incense, some myhr and some Channel Twenty-Two. The demonstration was very successful. The critics raved about it. And everyone understood how silly the Special Day Holiday proposal was, indeed.

And to this day there are seven people on the south side and one on E. 6th St. who still remember Jesus as he drove off in to the sunset yelling and waving his arms wildly. "Ho, ho, ho! And a very merry Special Day Holiday to you all!"

1970

FINDING IS LOST/LOSING IS FOUND

I hid
My love
'Neath the bough
Of a fair
Pine tree.
I do know where.

I hid
My love
Shouting,
"I'll never set
Foot there or I'll
Surely take root there!"
Be aware.

I hid
My love
And found
My fear
To be near
Only made me lonely
For the shade of
That fine pine bough.

So I went to where
That pine tree fair
Had been, but gone
Was the shade
That made the place
I hid
My love

So dear.

I played a while
And wept a tear
Forgot my fear
Only then, took root
But I still don't
Know where.

Devotion

Before the split
  There was one.
The split of me
  I stumbled upon so soon.
And yet it's been eternity
  In its coming.
I wanted to live in the clouds
  To live my dreams
To build an ideal, a Utopia
  In my mind
If only I could find
  The key.
I thought the key was me
  And I began to dig for it
So deep I couldn't sleep.

Well, I never did actually
Find the key, but I saw
It's shadow, but the shadow
Was not light and the
Light was through the door
And I had the key but I
Had no door and the door
Is you and the key is me.

I hope to see
  The door
    One day.

Come With Me

For all of my life
I have waited to love you.
All my life I have waited
For that moment
Only to find that the moment
Has passed in the waiting.

I can wait no longer
You are the object of my love
But I have no you, only love.
No longer is love in my heart
But I am in the heart of love.

No longer can I wait
I cannot hesitate
The moment that I want
Is passing me by
  I can fly
  I can fly.

You hold me in your arms
  I hold you
I see me in your smile,
  Only one.
I can taste your sweet, wet dew.
  I can feel
  Make me real.

Can It Be Me?

God is time
  How do you spend Him?
God is thought
  Do you know Him?
God is light
  What do you see?
God is everywhere
  Where are you?
God is love
  Are you lonely?
God in you
  Can it be?
God in me
  I can see the way.

Friday Night

My veil is so thin
And I'm not too sure
How to begin
To explain the things I see.

To free the spirit
Is to chain your soul
The light in the dark
Only illuminates illusion.

The key to real
Is in the feel
Feel the inside
And know the outside.

Know the inside and
Feel the outside
I reflect my environment
And it reflects me.

Let it bleed
Let it seed
Let it be.

Mr. Straight

If I could do things for you
To set you free, and you were me,
Would you see just what to do?

If I could show you the way
To let go of all you know
And simply flow, I would, today.

If you could see that I am you
And you are me, then you'd be
What you see in me. I'm you.

Then you'd see just what you need
And reach inside and find
You've nothing to hide. So be.

The world is yours and it's free.
You simply do whatever is you.
So reach in and see. Just be.

Now what I've said is in my head
Don't trust in me—I'm no authority
For if you do, you will be misled.

Use your eyes, look into the mirror
And see what you hear. The mirror is you
The mirror is me. Be free.

Everybody

The father:	The sum total of all Natural things outside Of myself.
The son:	Me, my body, the Temple Of the Lord.
The Holy Spirit:	The Soul or spirit of Humanity as a Whole.

All in the name of Love.

Children!

The shadow of the hand
Is among us now
Whispering the word
      We are the word
      You are the word
      I am the word.

The shadow of the hand
Is among us now
Showing the way
      I am the way
      You are the way
      We are the way.

Listen to it, seek it
Don't let them deceive you
For God will receive you
The shadow is back at last.

Comin' Home

And when I touch her hand
My heart throbs thump and pump
All the life-loving blood
 to my surface
And the surface, God,
 It's brewing a tempest storm
With waves a' rollin' and a' blowin'
  I'm flailing in my ship
  My stomach 'bout to rip.

And in my confusion
Amid the heat of transfusion
With fresh memories of lonesleeping
 I fear.
I am looking for the place
That will give me some space
Perhaps a cranny for a tear.

And that place is but a hum,
A droning hum among
The churlin' wheels in my ear.
And our eyes meet and
 our heartpounds beat
And in the the torrid confusion
I reach for the place
That's so dear.

And I speak a feint mumbling
And my head begins to bumbling
 for that place
It is true, it's confusion.

And she names it by name,
And it's delusion just the same
Brewing in a sea of dark shadows.

And so I'm comin' home again.
And so I'm comin' home.
And if anyone would ask
To where I have gone
Tell them I have gone
   to comin' home.

And when I look again
   I'm gone.
And I guess that I'm on my way.

1972

Huh?

A number of questions and problems have
arisen in my mind and body about relation-
ships in general and specifically. I feel certain
social pressures to sometimes act in a
manner contrary to personal definition.
I have demonstrated adequate control of
will to not be empirically effected by such
pressure, but I am aware of it nonetheless.
Simply by my thinking and, now, writing on
the subject I know that certain behaviors
are going to be changed. In the name of
personal development I feel it to be of
utmost importance to be at the helm when
entering choppy seas. I am not always
aware of what guides me or the goals of
the aforementioned. And being at the helm
does not necessarily indicate control, only
a good vantage point.

I think I see a star faintly flickering in
the night.

"It's all right," she said, "it's okay.
That star is not so far. Perhaps if you
quit looking for it the time will pass
more quickly until illumination gets
here. I looked at a similar light a long
time past. I looked high and low and when
it beheld me I looked deep. So deep that
I have seen nothing since; bright white
nothing," she quietly mumbled.

"It's all right," I said, but as I spoke
I looked around and nobody was there.

1972

Have you ever felt like a poet
and in trying to show it
you blow it?

1973

On Magic

The "how" of any particular process does
not necessarily describe what happens
within the process of any given effect,
or why; but rather it describes what is
done to influence the process. Take, for
example, making coffee: First, boil
water, then add crushed coffee beans, and
strain into a suitable container. Note
that nowhere in the procedural sequence
is included any description of "how" fire
heats water.

Let's, then, carefully describe "how" it
is that fire heats water. The fire causes
the water molecules to travel at an ever
increasing rate, eventually making bubbles
of steam rise from the bottom of the
suitable container. As it turns out, this
"fire (that) causes the water molecules
to travel at an ever increasing rate"
involves some sort of energy transfer
whose sole description is mathematical.

1973

Rock On

The difference is like that of touching
the table and feeling your finger tips;
or hearing the refrigerator and hearing
your ears; or seeing a sight and seeing
your vision—and from the other side,
it probably looks inside out.

1973

THE LAW OF UNIVERSAL WAR
OR THE WAR OF UNIVERSAL LAW

During before the beginning of
the beginning began to begin,
there always existed two opposites.
These opposites were sworn to
mutual opposite destruction,
which was derived from the
nature of the middle.
These extremes were so opposite
that they actually could not
determine the nature of the
middle, and that's what made
them so mad.
And they knew it! But it had
been going on since long before
the beginning even
began to begin. And at this
point they were not going to
turn back. I mean if they,
we, us, had come this far for
such a long time ... I mean, I
ask you: How could we stop it?

1973

64,000

The answer is:
  What is the question
And the question is:
  That is the answer
And that is: To the relationship
  as between
up or down or left or right
  and right only as in
the domain of perception
  be it inside or out,
and the key is relationship
  and within the universe
of discourse it does include,
of course,
everything!

1973

To Whom I May Concern:

Concerning the sanity of the aforesaid
constituent when involved in attempting
to reiterate a previous point of which
the aforesaid constituent has upon
several previous occasions been unable
to recount the circumstances under
which such point was mentioned is
hereby nullified.

Therefore, either the immediate phrasing
of that point of which the aforesaid
constituent has upon several occasions
been unable to recount is illusory, or
as is obvious by the account of the
immediate circumstance of the previous
occasion, it is not.

1973 or 74

So much has come
  yet, remains past.
I sit alone,
  no one home
I have come so far
  alone so far
      at home
      and yet
I can smell the dawn
  in my bones and
I love the taste and
  I can't stop thinking
of myself.

Clouds break into flowing
patterns of blue and
orange, swirling and
churning the dark of
night into the bright
white light of day.
Can you see beyond the
green of a tree, beyond the
blue yonder?—
Neither can I.

1974

Prolepses

I

There is a knowledge.
That knowledge is not
   clinging to ideas.
   But clinging to this
knowledge is not knowledge.

II

There is an idea.
That idea is not
   found anywhere,
   but the idea is
to find it.

III

There is a love.
That love is not
  loving ideas,
   but loving the
people who see them.

IV

These words are about thoughts.
Those thought are glimpses
   of fleeting ideas.
Anyone can see them.
   Everyone does see them,
      but no one knows
         what we see.

April 1974

Lost Again

Isn't it interesting,
not only that
you always find
whatever you're
looking for in the
last place that
you look, but that
whether or not
you find it depends
on whether you
concentrate on
looking or finding.

May 1974

Kidd Tit

Kid Tidd was not
  a big kid, tho'
her inside was
bigger 'n
her out.

It would be
  neater 'n
peaches and cream
  if it all
works out.

I'll probably jump
  and shout all
over the place
  for joy,
  oh boy.

Now, Kid Tidd was
  taller 'n she
was short, an'
  tho' I never was
a tit kid
  I found her heart
could warm my chest.

Tho' she seems a
  little thin, I'd
like to listen to
  her skin
and then …

> I'd probably jump
>   and shout all
> over the place
> for joy,
>   oh boy.

1974. In memory of Kit Tidd, who died too young.

When I look into my mirror
I know that the face I see
  is lonely,
Because the face that's
  looking is.
And it's only a mirror
  it's all a mirror.
What I see is me.

December 1974

Tune Up

She comes to me
  in paucity,
it seems—
  as tho' if in
a dream.

She has come to me
  in a dream,
it seems—
  as tho' if in
a veritable dream.

And when I awaken
  from a dream
like this
  I will go to her.
Yes, I will go.

And with her face
  in mine,
my hand in hers,
  I will look.
Oh, to chance a glance.

With my chin to
  the wind,
I'll see if I have
  anything to see,
anything to show.

She sees into me,

I look out
of her—
  We are always looking
for mine eye.

Come to me
  with none
of the dross of age,
  but with the
affirmation of faith.

Yes, with eyes
  to shine
like a time-lost star
  on a cold
winter night.

And I will
  burnish you
    with love.

January 1975

Some Koan

Is there a "the Truth"?
  Yes. And there isn't
    anything
   that it
doesn't mean.

November 1975

One X One / One = One

It takes
  a simple man
to sing
  a simple song.

O, the unity and
  the yangity.

Gosh,
  dad gum
dangity.

  Ain't it wonderfulity.

December 1974

Feelings hint—but
  the
   Tao
    know.

No Tao.
That's what
 the Tao know.

December 1974

Hoo?

Intellectual conceptualization
  and/or
conceptual intellectualization
  can't quite describe the
    all-of-it.
There's a residue—
  left.

Experience is broader
  yet, if ya' look ya' aughter'
see that in the *is*—er
  there is the *oughter.*
An' still
  there's a residue—
right?

As the limit of the residue
  approaches zero
The closer it gets to self.
  That is that
as the limit of the zero
  approaches the residue
the first thing it finds is
  self.

December 1974

A SKETCHY PORTRAIT OF A FAR-FETCHED, FRENZIED FOOL AS A FAR-OUT FELLOW

"A fool," some screamed silently to the others. A foolish acknowledgment glittered among those eyes whose inside was on the out, and versa visa—that is, that there was no difference betwixt those that thought the fool to be inside out and those who thought he was outside in.

"You fool," thought one, saying nothing. "The tools of your life are at hand! Give it up—come with us—join the band!"

The fool, on the other hand, thought that—not knowing it was the sound of his own wheels turning—he heard them saying, "The tools of your life are at your command. Give a damn!"

"The tools of my life," he pondered. "The tools of my life! Am I to understand that I am in command? Building my life? My God!? And if it's really true, then who are they and what do they wish me to build? And why?"

Having never before built a life, the fool that he was, he turned those very wheels to remembrance of faded images of those that had—and unintentionally—to those who had not.

Well, by this time it was plain to see for all who could see that nothing was going to be seen either from the inside or the out. And, thought the fool, from this time forward no one on the inside will ever look out, nor will those on the outside look in.

To the fool's dismay—which was exactly why he was referred to as a fool—those same outsiders, upon cognizing the condition of the one whose words so vindictively spewed from his mouth with no intentional direction, clasped the fool's mouth and forcing it open looked deep into the cavernous throat and with the aid of a small flashlight were able to detect an ever so slight palpitation.

"Such foolish words couldn't possibly have come from nowhere," thought one to himself.

"Even foolish ideas must have an origin," restated another to himself upon hearing the other.

Time was fast. Transportation machines hurriedly whizzed to and fro, fro and back. It was the dawn of an age that was about to dawn upon the rising of the sun. Dusk was gone. Dawn was coming and with that very dawn, slipping thru shadows of the early morning sun, were the words of a solemn gollum melting into light.

"Light!" shouted another. "More light!" The outsiders managed to amass not one but three working flashlights with which to illuminate the callous throat of the fool. "We must have more light," said three more in unison. "To the lawn, to the light of the dawn."

The three, with the inexhaustible help of two old ladies and a passing boyscout hoisted that same fool off of his ass and carried him upon their shoulders to the outside of the enclosure where they set him on the grass.

Meanwhile the fool, not wanting to taste those fumbling fingers which had previously pried into his words, decided while riding to the dawn to aid the outsiders when they reached the lawn. "Bring a mirror and an looking glass!" cried the fool.

"A mirror?" thought one young lass, while looking through her glass. "I'll just powder my nose and put on a face, should the dawn see me now 'twould be a disgrace. A mirror and a looking glass? How crass! The light of the dawn will shine upon that murmur in the base of that fool's throat and then we'll see what is to be seen, " she powdered.

Once upon the grass two men grabbed at his jowls and forced open the mouth of the fool in order to see the origin of the words that were the fool's only tools. But, lo and behold, the light of the dawn was blocked by the crowd on the lawn and only their shadows shown upon the jowls of the fool on the grass.

"No light," thought the two. "Now what'll we do?" And they released the one on the lawn.

Upon finding his jowls unharmed, the fool that he was, he cleared his throat. "Ah hem." The sound echoed through the caverns of his ears. Yet, the others could hardly hear.

"Perhaps with the aid of a mirror some light of the dawn could be reflected into the depths of my yawn," he mumbled.

A powdered nose from among the crowd held a mirror high above the shadows to reflect the now full-blown sun into that foolish yawn on the lawn. And the fool yawned a yawn long enough for all to see beyond the teeth. Each in turn saw, in the reflected light of the dawn, from whence came the words of the fool on the lawn.

As the last of the crowd gazed into the yawn, the powdered young lady, having stood so long, twitched just a bit and reflected the light of the dawn into the eyes of the fool commencing a yawn. As each in turn saw what was to be seen in the depths of the throat of the fool on the lawn, they went back in the building with good cheer and gleam, or so it would seem.

A young man was passing near the scene and having never before seen the fool, saw only a powdered nosed young lady holding a mirror high above her head, reflecting the light of the now full-blown day in the the eyes of a man on the lawn who was commencing a yawn.

"Good day," smiled the man to the two in the grass.

"Good day," mimicked the lady, and sat on her ass.

"Huh?" said the fool, not being able to spy for the light of the mirror had blinded his eye. "Good day to whomever I hear."

Then, turning in the direction of the young powdered voice, "Did you bring a looking glass?" He directed the question with his now cleared voice.

"A looking glass?" She smiled and blinked. Or was it a wink she blinked?

"A looking glass!" he said as he shook his head and looked with his eye toward the height of the sky. And they laughed and laughed in the full of the day.

Oh, and the month—it was May.

1974

The Obvious

Mr. B: Where have all my poems gone?
Mr. A: Where is the sun when it is not
eclipsed behind the moon?
Mr. B: Well, its slipping into or out of
various states of ordinarity. Why?
Mr. A: What poems?

March 1976

An Experience of Grace

The year was 1976. It was late August when I was going to graduate school at Colorado State University in Ft. Collins. It was dusk one evening. Dusk in Colorado always lingers late in to the evening because the sun sets behind the mountains, leaving that indirect dusklight clinging to nature like hoarfrost, and incandescently lighting up the sky.

I was sitting on the couch playing my guitar, staring glassy-eyed out the picture window which faced east, giving view to the distant horizon of the Great Plains. Melodye was across the room sewing.

As usual for that time of year the horizon had collected a herd of cumulus clouds, thunder clouds billowing high enough to tickle the heavens. It was still light enough to see the blue of the sky, but I imagine that if I had looked, I could have found a star. It was that instant between dusk and night.

Suddenly on the face of the clouds a flash of light, a red-orange brightness blossomed at ground level and climbed up the clouds illuminating for perhaps three full seconds the immense height of the billowing clouds. The absolutely astonishing thing about it was that the light originated from the ground level and climbed upwards.

"Melodye, look!" I gestured out the window as her head turned.

When the light had finally dissipated into the night we just sat there, alternately looking at each other and looking out the window. She looked a little pale; I felt very pale. For an instant I thought that we should go down to the basement before the shock wave hit us. I quickly estimated that it would take about 500,000 tons of TNT, or more likely, an atomic explosion to generate that much light.

I was afraid, afraid for my life. My heart and my imagination were racing frantically. I felt an intensity of the experience that I had only felt under fire in Viet Nam.

For a brief moment I knew that we had done it; the war was upon us. I knew that it had been inevitable, that we would blow ourselves up. What had happened? What went wrong? Why did this atomic war have to thrust itself into my life? I had no answers.

All of this happened in the space of about fifteen seconds. I had no choice but to resign myself to the acceptance that my life was about to end.

I knew that it had been a bomb. I knew of no reason that it should not have been. Lord knows that the international scene is drifting dangerously in that direction.

But there was no boom. No shock wave, no nothing. I turned on the TV to see what I could learn. Nothing.

Months later I found out that that year the Aurora Borealis, the Northern Lights, had been unusually active that year. They had been seen all over the world in places where they were rarely or never seen. I had never seen them before, but I saw them that evening.

But for me it was much more than just the Northern Lights. I had brought a lot to that experience. In the space of those fifteen seconds my whole life passed before me. And the whole history of the world passed before me. And as it passed I wondered, why not? Why wasn't it a bomb? Why haven't we blown ourselves up yet? What keeps us from doing it? God knows that we're ripe for it.

Then it occurred to me: it is really and truly by the grace of God that it was not an atomic bomb. We are literally living by the grace of God.

The world was saved by the grace of God that warm summer evening. But I died. In fact, the whole world died. Our graves are already marked. We died, and yet we are saved by God's grace.

My presence in seminary is a response to that grace. I carry that experience of grace with me now. And I am called to respond to it with the same intensity and continuity as it was shown to me.

So if anyone would ask, I would say, "Yes. I have seen the Aurora Borealis."

April 1978

The Confessional

I haven't been living in community. I don't know if I ever have. I'm not even sure I would recognize it if I saw it.

It's not necessary to live with other people per se, it can be done under any conditions. What it is? It's love. Love that people can share with themselves and others. What that love is cannot be defined because it isn't any particular thing. But what can be said of it is that God is the condition of its actuality, and reciprocally, love is the condition of God's existence. Love conceives God so that God may conceive more love. Someone said that there is only God—many before have also said this. But how can it be true? If there is only God, then there is also only love. Therefore, God equals love. And if my heart can be filled with love—whose condition is God—then it can rest in fullness, like a smoke after a huge meal, which has been ravenously consumed. So, if there is only God, then only I can only love only God.

All that's great, Father, but what ever happened to the specially loved person that I've been waiting for?

Quite frankly, the response came: You can only either seek God, or have found Him already. And it's your choice to make. God simply waits in eternal patience.

Alphalogos

Of a maiden,
Heaven born and
Fully awake.

A star in the
sky of mind.
Heaven sent and
Richly salient.

He is born
Yet unborn,
Eternally present.

October 1979

Cherries

The pits:
  kernels of resistance,
    hope of the blossoms,
      the root of regeneration.
Ambrosia!

May 1979

Christ Across!

We must Christ ourselves across
   The threshold of openhearted love
Or we may only be Christed
   To the doorway with help
But in either case we must
   bear the crossing ourselves.

We are called to follow Him
   Whose Christing crossed
     the threshold.

The strong Christ others,
   The weak can only Christ themselves.
The community Christs each other
   To the crossing of the threshold.

1979

Jesus' Prayer

Lord God who is heaven,
  Holy is your name.
Your kingdom is your will
  through the earthly
as the heavenly,
  now as forever.

Grant us daily the Life of our life.
Make us instruments of your
  inexhaustible forgiveness.

Lead us not into delusion.
  Deliver us from self-possession.

In Spirit and in Truth
  Thou art the Sovereignty
    and the Efficacy
      and the Excellence
        forever.
Amen.

June 1981

THE LORD ALSO SNOWS

Thus says the Lord:

I come to you as snow,
Living water blowing where I will,
On the wings of the Spirit.

I come to you as snow,
In the quiet of the night
For the beauty of the new morn.

My purity feeds your deepest springs,
And fills the wells from which you dip
The source of life.

I cleanse away the sins of iniquity,
And cover your folly
With a blanket of purity.

Who can face my brilliance
in the light of day?
Who is not overwhelmed by
my generous abundance?

But woe betide to the unprepared,
To whose who do not know my way,
Who will not heed my prophets.

I come to you gently in my season,
In beauty unsurpassed,
A beauty of consequent magnitude.

> I hide not my coming from you,
> Hide you not from my coming.

Published in the collection, *Daybreak on the Land*, The National Library of Poetry, 1997, "Editor's Choice Award," and in *Visions of Faith*, Triumph House, Peterborough, United Kingdom, 1998.

Written following an overnight three foot snow (average) in December 1996 in Central Pennsylvania. The title is a play on words from the praise chorus, *Our God Reigns*, Leonard E. Smith, Jr., New Jerusalem Music, 1974, 1978.

TRINITARIANISM

plurality <=> 1*1=1 <=> 1/1=1 <=> 3 <=> unity

Comprehend this: the God of plurality is singularly God.
    Love all parts as one.

The spirit is simultaneously product and quotient
    without confusion
        of thought, number, elements,
            kinds, types or phylum.

The father accounts for origin,
    the son for progeny,
        the spirit for unity.

The father originates,
    the son represents,
        the spirit authenticates.

Reality is a unitary complexity
    without confusion of elements
        nor derivative in design.

Life blooms.

(10/31/2010)

UNITARIANISM

zero <=> 0-0=0 <=> 1-1=0 <=> a-a=0 <=> unity

Dig it! God is the only.

Love is all in the head,
        all in the heart,
        all in the hand,
        all in the foot.

The spirit is unseen, undetectable, unknowable,
        the projection of subtraction,
                diversity without distinction,
                      nirvanic blandity.

The father is unaccountable,
        the son undiscernable,
                the spirit undifferientiatable.

Reality is an illusion,
        the illusion is real,
                nothing figures
                      but everything adds up
                              at the end.

Yet, god's calculation
        comes to the unity of all nothing,
                obedience to the death.

Blossoms die.

10/31/2010

www.ingramcontent.com/pod-product-compliance
Lightning Source LLC
Chambersburg PA
CBHW071331040426
42444CB00009B/2130